Baby Deltic

The Story of an Engine's Rebirth

Published by

The Baby Deltic Project

ISBN 978-0-9563127-0-9

Proof read by The Wordsmiths, thewordsmiths@hotmail.co.uk

Printed by Burgess Design and Print, Retford, Nottinghamshire.
Telephone: 01777 860579. www.burgessdesignandprint.com

Foreword

I am delighted and not a little flattered to be asked to write this foreword.

Simon, like me, is a product of the old B.R., so though a generation apart we are very much kindred spirits in matters diesel. I have worked with him professionally in the past, and know him as an eminently sound and capable engineer with a wealth of Deltic knowledge and 'hands on' experience. He has the drive and enthusiasm to succeed in things in which he believes, and a rare ability to lead and motivate others and overcome problems.

These attributes shine through in this, Simon's book about the Baby Deltic Project, telling the story of the only surviving T9-29 engine from Simon's finding it derelict and seized eight years ago, through its rebuild to a successful start-up and installation in a locomotive early in 2009.

The book is written from the heart – all true engineers have heart; they have real empathy for worthy machines above (almost) all else – and in a style that is easy to read, with illustrations accompanying the text giving clarity and helping to understand what was a complex and challenging undertaking. For those who want facts as well as drama, the appendices provide a wealth of technical detail and explanation.

Simon may feel that this is a specialist book with a limited potential circulation, but he may well be surprised. The 'down to earth' presentation of his and his team's achievements will, I think, broaden the book's appeal to include, in addition to the Napier devotees, diesel engine aficionados in general and also those interested in mechanical engineering and the wider railway. It is, after all, a piece of industrial archaeology.

I commend this book as a fascinating story of dedication, teamwork and triumph. It's a great read!

Neville Davies B.Sc., C.Eng., M.I.Mech.E.

Acknowledgements

No project of this magnitude can be undertaken without help. This help takes many forms – telephone calls made to ex-Napier personnel, the loan of tools and equipment, moral support when things are going badly.

Many people and companies have played their part in the return to operation of this unique piece of engineering heritage.

In the past I have shied away from listing people and organisations who have given assistance to the project for fear of causing offence by omission. However, with the caveat that I believe this list to be complete, I would like to thank, on behalf of the Baby Deltic Project, the following for their support in whatever form it has been given;

- The Deltic Preservation Society.
- Colchester Fuel Injection Ltd (Paul Goldsmith).
- The National Railway Museum (Helen Ashby).
- Rolls-Royce plc (Richard Haigh, Jim Vickerman, Graham Smith).
- MAN BW Ltd (Mike Gipson, Barry Cox).
- PW Fabrications Ltd (Phil Whetton).
- Barrow Hill Ltd (Mervyn Allcock).
- Pinza Ltd (John Campbell).
- Bralesford Engineering Services Ltd (Tim Bralesford).
- Harry Needle Railroad Company.

And the individuals;

- Mike Baker, Shaun Wright, James Williams, Steve Andrews, Colin Hartshorne, Jim Blake, Gavin Morrison, Andrew Wylie.

There is truly no doubt that without this assistance the project so far would have been significantly more difficult and far less enjoyable.

Throughout the book I have used photos from various sources, predominantly my own records. Where photographs are taken by others this is noted next to the photograph.

Simon Hartshorne
May 2009

(P)INDARI

We are delighted to support the restoration of this unique engine and lend our patronage to this fine book. The Baby Deltic Project had achieved much in simply returning the engine to running condition and they are to be congratulated. We wish them every success with their future ambitions and look forward to reading about the next steps in future books.

Well done!

Pindari Ltd is a consultancy to the rail industry providing;

- Compliance guidance and advice on Health and Safety legislation, Quality Management, Environmental legislation;
- Guidance and advice on traction and rolling stock engineering;
- Compliance guidance with legislation and railway group, ISO and EN standards;
- Competence management systems;
- Risk management;
- Project management.

The Managing Director served the rail industry for 24 years prior to leaving corporate employment with Network Rail to set up Pindari.

Recent contracts have been undertaken with a variety of rail industry suppliers and sub-contractors in the fields shown above.

We would like to discuss the ways we can help you achieve compliance, please contact us in the first instance at;

info@pindari.co.uk

(P)INDARI

Contents

Appendices

Introduction

The Baby Deltic Project was formed in 2002 to preserve and restore the last surviving engine from a Class 23 railway locomotive. It consists of a group of six enthusiasts with many years of Deltic experience between them. All of the original members were directly involved with the restoration of D9009 Alycidon, registering it and then operating it and 55019 Royal Highland Fusilier on main line metals. Following on from this was the construction of the DPS Depot at Barrow Hill Roundhouse near Chesterfield. There was little doubt therefore that these people had the ability to project manage and carry out an effective refurbishment of the T9-29 engine.

The group's first job, after acquiring the engine from the National Railway Museum, was to move it to a more secure environment. Over the years, residing in the open air at the back of the NRM and exposed to the elements the tarpaulin covering the engine had decayed and allowed the atmosphere to start to cause damage.

The newly purchased engine was moved from York to MAN BW Ltd at Colchester in January 2002 where it rested for eighteen months drying out. In September 2003 the engine was moved to the DPS Depot where it remains to this day.

This book is not a treatise on the history of the Class 23 locomotives. Rather, it describes the trials and tribulations of returning this unique engine back to working order. In order to carry out such a project in amongst group members' work, other Deltic activities, hobbies and of course personal life a huge amount of planning and organization has taken place. For example, removing the commutator from a generator is not a one man job. It takes a lot of effort. Similarly the bringing together of materials required for a specific day was essential. If it was operated on the 'hobby' side of railway preservation the Group would never have achieved the progress it did. By taking a professional approach to the project BDP has achieved what many people said was impossible.

So far this project has been self financed. In purchasing and reading this book you are helping the BDP to achieve its next goal. The target of having a T9-29 operating in a railway locomotive once more is a challenging and expensive one. You can help to achieve this by telling your friends about the Baby Deltic Project and persuading more people to buy this book and support our fundraising activities. All profits from sales will go directly towards the project. By making a donation to the Baby Deltic Project you can rest assured that all monies will go directly into getting the engine and donor locomotive running once more. Please attend the events organized by the Baby Deltic Project, Deltic Preservation

Society and Barrow Hill Roundhouse. You will have the opportunity to see how we are progressing and, of course, be able to drop a bit of the folding stuff into our donation bucket! If you work for, or know of, a Company that you think could help us either with materials, expertise or sponsorship then please let us know. If you or anyone you know is willing to help us, we will be able to further our aims, possibly even see a Baby Deltic hybrid hauling trains.

Keep in touch, or make a donation, by visiting our website at;

www.thebabydelticproject.co.uk

Or contact us by writing to us at;

The BDP, c/o Barrow Hill Roundhouse, Campbell Drive, Staveley, Chesterfield, S43 2PR.

Research for a definitive book about the history of the Class 23 locomotive, the development of the T9-29 engine and of course what has happened since this engine was installed in a donor locomotive is presently underway. In many ways its content is once again down to you helping us. A lot of the ground has already been covered. By buying this book, making a donation or putting us in touch with people who can help you can contribute to our success.

Additionally if you know of anyone who has any experience of, or information about, the development of the locomotive, its introduction, service history or demise then we would love to hear from you. Any additional information and photographs we can obtain will help us piece together a more complete history of this unique locomotive.

We hope that you enjoy reading about the Baby Deltic Project. Within these pages you will read what it means to bring a Deltic engine back to life. Similarly, and for the first time, you will read about how and what goes into making a Deltic engine work. We hope you find it interesting; it has been a fascinating process for us to bring this story together for you. Things have come a long way for the Baby Deltic Project since the engine was acquired in 2002. Looking forward we still have much to do to enable enthusiasts to experience this engine in action once more, why not be part of it?

Nigel Paine
June 2009

Chapter one
Discovery

The story of this power unit has been the subject of some considerable investigation details of which were still being uncovered at the point of printing. Our engine (serial number 388) was the last of the T9-29 type built for British Railways by D. Napier & Son (by now owned by English Electric) at Netherton, Liverpool in 1957. It was built as a spare engine – sixteen engines being ordered as part of the contract to supply ten locomotives. The first official record of the engine available to date was its installation in D5905 on the occasion of the locomotives refurbishment by English Electric. The locomotive arrived at Doncaster on 29 November 1964 and was released to traffic following acceptance trials on 18 December.

By 5 May 1966 the engine had accumulated 4000 hours – the contract overhaul life. D5905 returned to Doncaster where the engine was removed and sent for overhaul at the Napier Works. After overhaul it was installed to D5909 which was released from Doncaster on 15 November 1966. Just over a year later, on 11 December 1967, D5909 failed with a defect on B3 inlet piston and was hauled to Doncaster where the engine was removed and sent to Napier for repair. Once repaired engine 388 was installed once more to D5905 and released to traffic on 18 December 1968. D5905 was withdrawn on 11 February 1971 with a failed auxiliary gearbox shaft and was sent (on 12 March 1971) to Stratford Diesel Repair Shop (DRS) where the power unit, traction motors and steam generator were removed.

D5905 (and D5909 which had joined '05 at Stratford) were sent for disposal at G Cohen's, Cransley in August 1973. The power unit from D5905 remained in a wagon covered with a tarpaulin as a spare for D5901, which had found further use with the Railway Technical Centre after the end of its BR career. Unused, and unwanted after the withdrawal of D5901, the spare engine was claimed by John Bellwood of the NRM on 29 March 1977 and delivered to York on 16 August 1977 at a cost of £164.77.

Moving forward to 2001, there had previously been publicity about a proposed project to create a replica version of the English Electric Type 2 using a power unit purchased from the NRM. It appeared, however, that very few people had actually seen the engine in question.

After a tip off from NRM staff, we went on a voyage of discovery. The engine was allegedly in a secondary store location within the NRM inaccessible to the general visitor. However, the recent clearing of the old British Telecom Telephone Engineering Centre on Leeman Road to make way for new houses allowed us to get alongside the fence to this storage area. Not immediately obvious due to the removal of the crankcase cover and its generally care worn appearance but there, in the distance, in a 5-plank wagon, beneath a very degraded tarpaulin, was what appeared to be the sole remaining T9-29 engine, ex-Class 23 'Baby' Deltic with its generators and governor. The true condition would not be discovered until later.

Back at the NRM, investigation of an aerial photo in the staff reception indicated that the power unit had been in the same location for some time -the photo showed yellow BT vans parked in, at that time, an extant BT TEC. It never occurred to me that the engine would still be stored outside and now so exposed to the atmosphere. If the power unit was still here, I figured that meant that it probably hadn't been sold and that in turn meant that it might still be available.

Discovery!   Photo: Richard Senior

Almost immediately I began a dialogue with the museum to ascertain the ownership status of the engine and, subsequently, whether there was any chance of it being sold to us. I was pleasantly surprised to learn that the museum believed that engine was still owned by them, the previous sale having fallen through. They agreed to look deeper into the actual position of the sale and promised to get back to me 'soonest'. Some months passed before I was contacted again with the information that the previous sale had never been completed and the question posed, "would I like to buy the engine?" Rashly (in retrospect) I offered to pay the same amount for the engine as was offered by the previous prospective purchaser, without knowing what this amount was. Within days a letter from the Curator of Collections was received and I learnt that I had bought a piece of history. The letter contained two caveats;

1. That the sale was contingent on us restoring the engine – or at least not allowing further deterioration, and,
2. That we should remove it as soon as possible.

At the time, we had regular contact with MAN BW Ltd. (formerly Paxman Diesels) in Colchester – they had the contract for repair and overhaul of Deltic engines for the Royal Navy (of types 9-55B and 9-59K) for the Hunt Class Mine Counter-Measures Vessels (MCMV), it occurred to us that they might be prepared to store the engine in the short-term. They might also be interested in investigating the condition of it. These questions were asked and answered in the form; "Yes" and "Don't be cheeky", in that order!

388, just arrived at MAN BW Ltd, Colchester   *Photo: Colin Hartshorne*

During the time the engine spent in Colchester, various fund-raising options were investigated to enable us to instruct MAN BW to undertake – at the very least – an investigation of the condition of the engine. In the event these options came to nothing although MAN did use a hand turning ('barring-over') tool in an attempt to get the crankshafts to rotate, unsurprisingly they remained resolutely stuck - the engine was seized solid.

The irony of this statement was only fully revealed much later in the project when it was discovered that every internal surface of the engine was coated with inhibiting oil. This can only have been done if the engine was inhibited 'according to the book', i.e. after a period of running. The implication here is that the engine was stored after its final run in a fully operational condition and had some low-life not stolen the crankcase covers (presumably for 'enthusiast display' rather than scrap – there was no sign of stud pulling or sawing through bolts) at some point in the engine's history there would have been every chance of its running virtually ex-store.

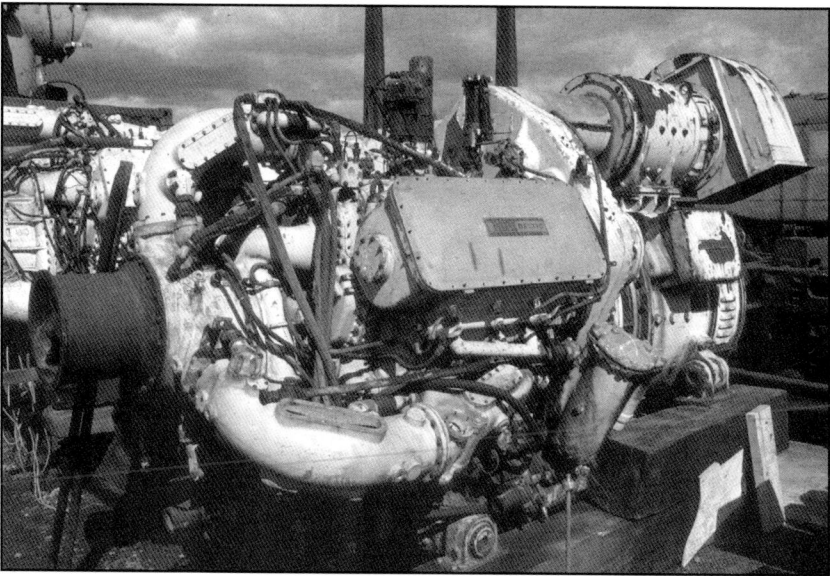

Engine 388 after arrival at the newly-built DPS Depot at Barrow Hill. It now carries two new crankcase covers kindly donated by MAN BW Ltd.   *Photo: Richard Senior*

The photograph above shows the power unit standing outside again, after some 18-months in the warm and dry in Colchester. Its external sojourn was short-lived and lasted only until the new DPS Depot was complete, moving in the week leading up to the grand opening ceremony on 20 September 2003. Just visible in the background is a T18-37K Deltic engine ex-Royal Norwegian Navy 'Nasty Class' Fast Torpedo Boat.

Clearly seen in this photograph is the highly unusual (for other than a shunting locomotive) arrangement of the fan for providing cooling air to one pair of the traction motors being overhung from the auxiliary generator. In similar fashion to the bigger D18-25B engines, the auxiliary generator is mounted on top of the main generator and is driven by a separate shaft from the phasing gear case.

At this time there was no intention to do anything other than 'preserve' the engine - in whatever yet-to-be-agreed form that would take. All the members of the 'Baby Deltic Project', as it had come to be known, were (and still are) members of the Deltic Preservation Society so the invitation to store the engine within the DPS Depot was easily achieved; almost a formality.

The assistance (both visible and invisible) given to the project by the DPS cannot be underestimated and to the Society above all others we extend our heartfelt gratitude.

Chapter two
Initial work

For a couple of years after moving into the DPS Depot, time pressure on project members prevented any real work from being undertaken on our engine – other than the liberal application of penetrating oil on exposed machined surfaces, fasteners which might one day require undoing and into the cylinder bores. In the photograph above the power unit sits between two 18-cylinder variants of Deltic engines, on the left a D18-7A ex-'Ton Class' Minesweeper HMS Wilton (the first 'plastic warship') and on the right a T18-37K.

Progress at the point this picture was taken (February 2007) was limited to removal of the combined traction motor blower and auxiliary generator – necessary to get the engine to fit through the Depot door – and removal of the exhaust manifolds, which can be seen lying beside the engine. The exhaust manifolds were removed in an attempt to get penetrating oil deep inside both ends of the cylinders.

The main generator is sitting on temporary wooden stands in readiness for its separation from the engine later the same week when work commenced in earnest.

At first glance the picture below appears to be the same as the one on the previous page, closer examination shows that the main generator has now been separated from the engine. The process of generator removal is relatively simple with a flange-mounted machine such as this, especially with a suitable overhead crane – which we didn't have. Instead, having uncoupled and supported the generator input flange on a bespoke armature support bracket, uncoupled the two-piece adapter ring and removed two-piece generator cooling fan, the generator was jacked up slightly to allow machine skates to be placed under the transport mounts (which are just visible at the 6 o-clock position).

The engine – now supported on more robust mounts and in four places so as completely to prevent rocking – remained in place whilst the generator was drawn away, slowly. The whole process from uncoupling to completion took in the order of three hours, great care being taken throughout, especially as the wheels of the skates crossed the rail flangeways in the concrete floor of the Depot.

Once clear of the engine the generator was jacked again to remove the skates and to allow packing to be removed so that the generator could rest closer to the floor. This was in order to mitigate the risk of it rocking and falling off the mounts whilst work was undertaken on it - the stability of the generator was potentially reduced once it was separated from the engine.

Above: An unusual photograph taken from above after the main generator had been removed, looking down on 'B' bank.

Below: 'A' bank exhaust ports after the manifold was removed.

Chapter three
Starting work in earnest

With both generators removed, a further (predictably futile) attempt was made to turn the engine, just in case it was either machine causing the seizure. Of course it wasn't, but, faced with the massive task of a complete strip and rebuild it was worth a final try.

The photo below is of 'AB' crankcase, which contains 'AB' crankshaft and its torsional vibration damper, with four of the six (nos. A1 inlet, A2 inlet, B1 exhaust and B2 exhaust) connecting rods disconnected and pushed into their respective cylinders. The picture also shows (clockwise from top left) the phasing case, the pneumatically controlled, hydraulically operated engine governor and load control assembly, 'B' bank exhaust elbow ('B' bank exhaust manifold already removed), part of the turbocharger, the engine air intake and the crankcase breather hose. The pipe with three stubs below the crankcase is a drain oil manifold from the crankcase.

Appendix one at the back of this book contains a description of the layout and basic operation of Deltic engines.

Baby Deltic Project

ID	Task Name	% Complete	Start	Finish	
1	Baby Deltic project	97%	Mon 12/02/07	Fri 28/03/08	£3,911.00
2	Failed	100%	Mon 12/02/07	Mon 12/02/07	Failed
3	Running	90%	Fri 28/03/08	Fri 28/03/08	Running
4	Engine	100%	Tue 13/02/07	Fri 28/03/08	£100.00
28	Phasing case gearbox	100%	Fri 23/03/07	Mon 16/04/07	£0.00
39	Generator (main)	100%	Mon 12/02/07	Thu 27/03/08	£20.00
53	Generator (aux)	94%	Mon 12/02/07	Tue 20/02/07	£0.00
62	T/M blower	92%	Mon 12/02/07	Mon 19/02/07	£0.00
69	Turbo	100%	Fri 09/03/07	Fri 16/03/07	£0.00
76	Sandwich piece	100%	Fri 09/03/07	Tue 13/03/07	
80	Auxiliaries	99%	Tue 13/02/07	Wed 19/03/08	£2,040.00
173	Mounting feet	100%	Wed 14/02/07	Mon 19/02/07	
178	Mods	0%	Mon 12/02/07	Mon 12/02/07	£250.00
161	Additions / requirements	83%	Mon 12/02/07	Thu 27/03/08	£1,200.00
197	VDA	70%	Fri 21/12/07	Fri 28/03/08	£301.00

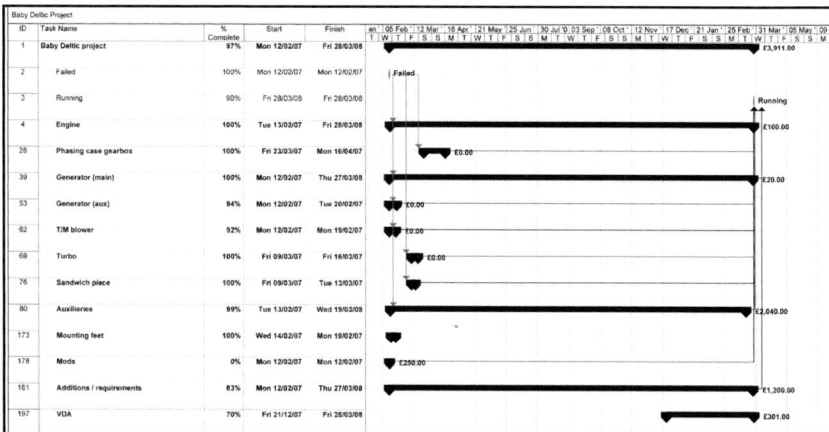

A programme of works was drawn up which comprised a project plan and quality plan. Throughout the refurbishment attention to detail was key – Deltic engines are not simple machines and errors needed to be avoided. The quality plan ran to several pages and took the form of a 'track and prompt' paperwork trail to ensure that no work requirement on any component would be overlooked at any stage of the refurbishment.

babydeltic project
quality, repair, inspection and test plan
issue 2
sheet no: 3 of 13

babydeltic t9 29

Ref.	Component	Activity	Document / other	Assessment / demonstration criteria	Authority BDP	Authority Other
Disassemble, inspect and overhaul phase						
1.	**Power unit, complete**					
1.1	Power unit, complete	Inspect, initial	None		WS	S
2.	**Dismantle power unit**					
2.1	Generators	Remove	None		WS	S
2.2	Phasing case	Remove	None		WS	S
2.3	Turbo	Remove	None		WS	S
2.4	Sandwich piece	Remove	None		WS	S
3.	**Engine**					
3.1	Pistons and rods	Remove	None		WS	S
3.2	Crankshafts	Remove	None		WS	S
3.3	Engine triangle	Pressure test – cold	No leaks at 5 psi (ambient)		WS, A2	W
3.4	Engine triangle	Pressure test – hot	No leaks at 5 psi (50°C)		WS, A2	W
3.5	Pistons	Clean	None		WS, A2	W
3.6	Pistons	Inspect	See WS		IRS, A2, X	S
3.7	Engine triangle	Oil flow test	See WS		WS, A1	H
3.8	Connecting rods	Inspect	See WS		IRS, A3	W

Key
H - Hold point
S - Surveillance
W - Witness
WS - Work sheet
R - Required
None - Use best practice

A1 - 100% inspection
A2 - Sample inspection
A3 - Final assembly inspection
AP - External approval required
IRS - Inspection report sheet
CoC - Certificate of conformance

MC - Material certificate
X - Documentation required for lifetime quality records pack

More important than anything else at this stage, the scope was determined; "To investigate the possibility of a return to operational condition of the sole remaining T9-29 Deltic engine and its generators."

Chapter four
Main Generator

In the same approximate sequence of tasks followed by the project, the following chapters detail the work involved in the refurbishment of the power unit [1] starting with the main generator.

After separation from the engine the complete main generator was turned through 90° to allow the removal of the armature. This was no mean feat as the armature is free to move both longitudinally and laterally at one end and required considerable mechanical restraint to prevent inadvertent (and dangerous) early separation. Once secured in an upright position, and with its bearing retaining bolts removed, the armature could be lifted out of the carcase.

The two parts are seen shortly after dismantling. The armature, seen to the rear in this photograph, is virtually all copper and the carcase (containing the field coils) virtually all iron.

The complete assembly weighs around three tonnes and accounts for over a third of the total weight of the power unit. The scope for refurbishment included a thorough clean, painting of field coils and cabling with anti-track varnish, insulation testing, continuity testing, testing of field coil ohmic values, repair or renewal of cables as required and refurbishment of brush holders including spring renewal and renewal of brushes.

---

(1) The terms 'power unit' and 'engine' are not interchangeable. Power unit refers to the assembly of engine and its main and auxiliary generators. The engine is the power unit without the generators.

Above: The armature, complete with the bearing retaining cap, is pictured lying on a pallet after its final clean.

Below: The carcase after a final application of anti-track varnish.

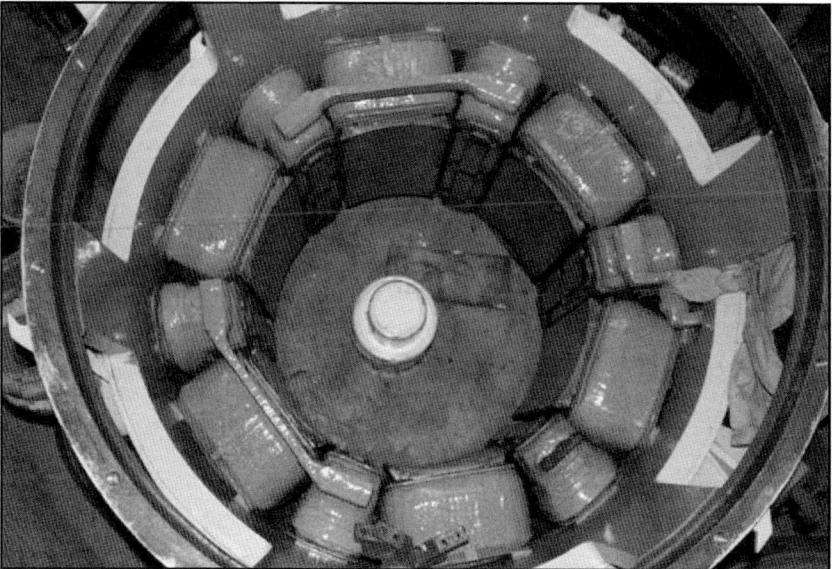

(Left) A photograph looking into the main generator showing a brush box prior to refurbishment.

A DC machine such as this is continuously rated at high rotational speed (1600 rpm maximum – the same as the engine speed), high voltage (400v) and high current (1700 amps). The relationship between volts and amps is directly proportional (as Ohm discovered) so the voltage can be much higher than its continuous rating.

Conditions such as this require a machine which is extremely robust. Cleanliness is also essential.

Considering the time spent stored in far from ideal conditions this view isn't too disappointing.

In Richard Senior's photograph (right) the main generator armature is lowered into the carcase after both items have been refurbished.

This was a skilled process with careful alignment of the end-plate bearing required to ensure that neither the armature nor the bearing was damaged during reassembly.

The other skilled process was rotating the assembled machine through 90 degrees without the armature moving out of alignment – a task made considerably easier by the use of the overhead crane in the HNRC workshops next door.

The post refurbishment photograph seen above shows the results of a complete strip and tens of man-hours of cleaning. The brushes, brush springs, bolts and insulators are all new. The commutator has been thoroughly cleaned, polished, undercut and dressed and checked to ensure that the connection relationship between each commutator bar is correct. The current collector ring has been thoroughly cleaned and repainted. The entire internal surface of the main generator carcase has been thoroughly cleaned and repainted.

Chapter five
Turbo and sandwich piece

The use of a turbocharger in engines for rail applications is commonplace; the use of a turbocharger of this design is – so far as I am aware – unique. Most turbos use exhaust gases alone as the driving medium[1] whereas Napier used a design for Deltics where the turbo is driven by two shafts, one each from 'AB' and 'BC' crankshafts, passing back through the engine to a speed raising gearbox mounted on the turbo in exactly the same fashion as the simpler (and more common) scavenge-blower arrangement. The turbo difference comes into effect at higher engine output when the exhaust gasses act on a driving turbine and begin to relieve the drive load on the drive shafts.

The turbo can be seen clearly in this photograph, as can the exhaust elbows from 'B' and 'C' cylinder banks.

The turbo exhaust section, previously removed as part of investigations to ensure that the engine seizure wasn't caused by the turbo, is lying on the floor adjacent to the engine.

(1) General Motors (EMD) engines used in Classes 59, 66 and 67 use a similar arrangement to Deltics except that the turbo is driven by the engine at low speeds but 'breaks free' via a dog-clutch at higher speed to act as a 'pure' turbo.

Two hours after the previous photograph was taken, the turbo (part of which is just visible on the extreme left) has now been removed and leaves the sandwich piece exposed. The two gears which drive the speed raising gearbox can now be seen just in board of the top two crankcase end-covers.

The speed raising gearbox is mounted on the engine side of the turbo. Its driven gears can just be seen through the apertures at approximately 9 o'clock and 3 o'clock.

Meshing of these gears is a critical part of the rebuild / assembly process; the Napier Training Notes leave the engine builder in little doubt as to the possible ill-effects of not following instructions to the letter.

Also clearly visible in this photograph are the three oval shaped air intake ducts – one for each cylinder bank – and the bearing housings for the gears within the speed raising gearbox.

(Right) The turbocharger before any cleaning took place.

The free end is to the left, the exhaust section was removed before the turbo was separated from the engine, the turbine disc can be seen on the left of this photograph.

The exhaust entry (from 'C' cylinder bank) is clearly seen, the much smaller pipe stub above it is the coolant connection between the turbo and 'C' bank exhaust elbow / manifold assembly.

The exhaust section (left hand side) and the air section (right hand side) are clearly identifiable.

(Left) Seen again after cleaning.

The flexible pipes would all be renewed prior to completion of the refurbishment.

Just visible, mounted on the centre right of the turbocharger is the metering oil pump. This pump is driven by an eccentric lobe off the speed raising gearbox. It takes a feed from the main engine oil gallery (via a filter), reduces the oil flow to around 330 cc per hour, and feeds it to the turbo bearings.

Priming of this pump is critical in the early stages of engine running and testing.

Chapter six
Phasing case

The unique Deltic arrangement of three crankshafts in triangular arrangement gives rise to the similarly unique arrangement of a phasing gearbox ('phasing case'). Apart from combining the drives from three crankshafts to a common output, the phasing case serves several other purposes; providing a drive output to the auxiliary generator, providing a drive output to the engine governor and overspeed and underspeed devices, providing drives for the pressure and scavenge oil pumps, and (on other applications other than this) drives for cooling fans and hydraulic clutch pumps. The gears in the phasing case can be arranged (at the design stage) to raise or lower the output shaft speed relative to the crankshaft speed. For example, whereas the D18-25B engine fitted to Class 55 locos has a generator which turns at ¾ the speed of the crankshafts, our engine (in common with the Deltic Prototype loco) is arranged so that the generator turns at engine speed.

Photo: Richard Senior

This photograph shows the phasing case after splitting. The output to the main generator is driven off a flange mounted shaft attached to the centre gear. The crankshaft gears are not fitted but their idlers can be seen (one idler each for 'AB' and 'BC' crankshafts, two for 'CA' which rotates in the opposite direction) as can the oil pump drive gears in the bottom corners.

(Left) The other half of the phasing case showing the three crankshaft drive gears absent from the previous picture. The gears are heat shrunk onto the quillshafts and are too large to pass through the bearing housings, hence the reason why they stay in the gearbox.

The gear at the top of the case is the auxiliary generator drive.

(Below) The two halves of the phasing case are brought together for reassembly. Each gear rotates in its own bearing with no play and therefore virtually no lateral movement. Alignment of the gears with the relevant bearings to close the case is, therefore, tricky. On this engine it took nearly two hours and several attempts.

Throughout the phasing case, and also in the free-end gearbox, there are a number of 'sparge-jets'.

These are critical in the lubrication of the gears – there being no sump for gear oil as in a conventional gearbox.

Each jet assembly has two or three (depending on location) tiny holes drilled into a machined face and is arranged to spray oil direct onto the gear.

As with so many seemingly minor components on the engine, the importance of their cleanliness cannot be understated.

Four of the sparge jets within the phasing case.

The larger gear at the top of the photograph is the output gear (to the main generator).

Note again the two idler gears for 'CA' crankshaft gear (missing, at the bottom) which rotates in the opposite direction to 'AB' and 'BC' crankshaft.

Both photos this page: Richard Senior

Chapter seven
Triangle

This picture ably demonstrates why the bare engine is referred to as the 'triangle'. With the turbocharger and sandwich piece removed from the free end[1] of the engine and the phasing case removed from the drive end the contents of the unseen part of the engine are revealed – some cylinder block coolant vent hoses and fresh air!

The apertures in the ends of each of the crankcases take the crankshaft quillshafts. These transfer the drive from each crankshaft into the phasing case. The circular covers inboard of these apertures retain the gears which drive the shafts for the turbocharger (from 'AB' and 'BC' crankshafts) and the free end gear box (from 'CA' crankshaft).

Lying horizontal on top of 'B' bank is the overspeed trip cylinder. This should be attached to the phasing case but was damaged during the movement of the engine onto the 'Warflat' carrier vehicle.

---

(1) The free end is the end of the engine opposite to the end from which the drive is taken, regardless of whether it is actually 'free', or not. British convention is to identify components relative to the free end, American convention is the reverse.

One of the most important jobs – and earliest in the programme – was to ensure that the cylinder liner seals and other internal coolant passages were secure and free from leaks. To do this, the engine was filled with coolant (a 30% solution of anti-freeze in softened water) and heated before gently increasing the water pressure. This picture shows the coolant at a temperature of 58.9°C. An engine should never be pressure tested cold as this can easily cause damage to seals and hoses. Although the Napier Training Notes call for significant pressure to be applied during the test, we took the pragmatic approach that 20 psi (approximately four times normal operating pressure) for sixty minutes without loss would suffice. The pressure test passed without leaks.

The triangle, now sitting on its new mounting feet, sits in the VDA. At this point it had been thoroughly degreased, hot washed, dried and petrol washed. The same treatment had been applied to all surfaces, internal and external to guarantee so far as possible that the engine was scrupulously clean prior to rebuild.

The internal coolant vent hoses would be renewed before reassembly could begin.

Comparison between this photograph and the one on page 30 goes some way to show the level of cleaning required throughout the project – in the order of 200 man-hours on the triangle alone.

Chapter eight
Exhausts, oil pumps and auxiliaries

Not, perhaps, the most exciting chapter title – or indeed the most interesting part of the refurbishment - it was essential nonetheless. The exhaust manifolds on a Deltic are cooled by a jacket through which engine coolant is circulated. The result of this is that oil passed from the cylinders is not burnt off immediately and tends to collect in the system. Deltics pass large amounts of oil by virtue of having exhaust ports in the cylinder walls and a not particularly good oil scraper ring design[1]. Over time this oil solidifies and coagulates to form a tarry substance. There is a danger that if not removed this tar can ignite and cause significant damage to the engine. In normal service the oil burns off in small quantities when the exhaust gas temperature gets high enough – this results in the classic 'Deltic exhaust', photographs of which abound.

B bank exhaust manifold before cleaning.   *And after.*

---

(1) This design has been vastly improved by Rolls-Royce in their work with the Royal Navy Deltics.

Being of triangular form Deltic engines are a little top heavy. In order to keep the engine height and therefore the centre of gravity to a minimum they do not have a conventional sump into which the oil drains and is stored; instead a separate tank is employed. The use of a tank requires two pumps where a conventional oil system uses just one; there is a pressure pump which takes oil from the oil tank and pressurises it to allow lubrication of the engine. From the various galleries within the engine gravity returns the oil to 'CA' crankcase, from where the scavenge pump draws it via a strainer and a thermostatically controlled oil cooler back to the oil tank. Both pumps are located on the engine side of the phasing case *(q.v.)*, one either side of 'CA' crankcase.

This is the oil scavenge pump seen before removal from the phasing case.

On top of the pump is the hose which carries the oil from the pump to the cooler from where it returns back to the tank.

Slightly above and behind that hose is a centrifugal air separator – oil is pumped round the perimeter of a cylinder and, being heavier than air, is separated from air bubbles within it. The air escapes to atmosphere through a vent – not shown here.

The oil filter housing is the cylindrical object above the pump.

The same pump after thorough cleaning and inspection mounted back on the phasing case. The 8-hole cover retains the strainer ('chip trap') which prevents stray metallic particles re-entering the oil system – examination of the strainer is a maintenance requirement and provides early warning of catastrophic engine failure. The union above the pump is for the oil priming connection.

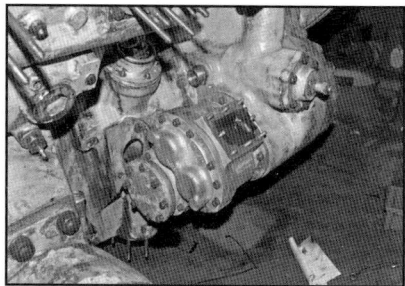

Mention was made earlier of the free-end gearbox. This is gear driven by a shaft off 'CA' crankshaft which – exactly like the drive for the turbocharger – passes along the length of the engine, this time within 'CA' crankcase. The purpose of the free-end gearbox is to drive the coolant circulating pump and (when the engine was installed in the locomotive) to drive the auxiliary gearbox, which itself drove the radiator cooling fan and the air compressor.

Seen above before any work was undertaken on it is the free-end gearbox, the coolant circulating pump is to the left and the coupling for the auxiliary gearbox drive to the right. The canister to the right of the auxiliary gearbox coupling is the fuel filter housing; the component partially obscuring the coolant circulating pump is the coolant flow switch.

This switch was retro-fitted by English Electric when the locomotives were refurbished; one of the problems with the locos as-built was that the auxiliary gearbox drive shaft would break, flailing around in the process and destroying anything in its path. Of the items in its path, the closest are the coolant pipes which, once fractured, drain the coolant out of the engine at a substantial rate. The engine would only shut-down once sufficient coolant had drained out of the header tank to operate the low-level switch by which time significant engine damage had usually occurred. The coolant flow switch monitors the flow of coolant by pressure differential and acts to shut down the engine as soon as detection is lost, i.e. immediately that a pipe is fractured.

Chapter nine
Pistons and crankshafts

There is no cylinder head on a Deltic engine, compression being achieved by opposed pistons. One piston is arranged at either end of the cylinder. Therefore, in order to remove the pistons, the crankshafts must first be removed. Ordinarily this operation presents little difficulty but with a seized engine such as this it presented a considerable challenge.

The picture on page 18 shows the crankshaft in position. This picture (looking into the crankcase at B2 exhaust and C2 inlet con-rods) demonstrates the confined space inside the crankcase.

Normally the crankshafts would be rotated to bring the big-end nuts to a convenient position where they can be undone. With the engine seized this cannot be done and several hours, considerable patience and not inconsiderable ingenuity were needed to disconnect all the big end nuts – each of which is secured by a (rusted in) split pin.

Once disconnected, and if they were free, the pistons could be pushed deep into the cylinders to make room for the removal of the crankshaft. For the pistons that were seized it was necessary to leave them in position and work round the problem.

The difficulties with crankshaft removal were not confined to big-end disconnection. As described on page 27, the drive from the crankshafts to the phasing case is by quillshafts which are retained, by a large ring nut, to the end of the crankshaft. This ring nut in turn is locked to prevent loosening in service by means of a locking lug and tab-washers. The engine seizure necessitated the undoing and removal of these locking devices in whatever position they came to rest – not easy.

With the big-ends and quillshafts disconnected the main bearing caps could be removed leaving, at last, the way clear to lift out the crankshafts.

The photograph below is of 'BC' crankcase after the crankshaft had been lifted out. On the far right of the crankcase is the quillshaft gear which mates with the crankshaft as previously described. The items which appear to be cut pieces of garden hose are exactly that - placed over the main bearing cap studs to prevent damage during crankshaft removal.

The difficulties presented by the top two crankshafts faded into simplicity when compared with the bottom ('CA') one. All of the problems encountered were repeated here with the added bonus of having to work lying on the floor.

The proximity of the components to one's body caused by the lack of clearance between the floor and the bottom of the engine meant that you could either see what you were doing, or do it, but certainly not both at the same time.

Furthermore, the effects of gravity meant that removing the crankshaft was extremely awkward – a special cradle was made to hold the crankshaft as it was lowered out of the crankcase; without this it would have been virtually impossible, not to mention dangerous.

With all three crankshafts out we were able to assess their condition and were pleasantly surprised with the result.

Apart from some surface corrosion on the balance weights, webs and torsional vibration dampers they were undamaged. Certainly the critical areas – the big-end and main bearing surfaces – were spotless, protected all these years by a film of lubricating oil.

This picture is of the three crankshafts on their specially made cradles, designed to prevent instability and bending during cleaning and storage. The outer two are 'AB' and 'BC' respectively; the centre is 'CA'.

The difference in appearance is testament to the destructive effects of the atmosphere during the time the engine was stored with the crankcase covers missing, 'CA' crankshaft being considerably better protected.

The large circular object on the end of each crankshaft is a torsional vibration damper, being necessary to reduce the effects of the impulses caused as each cylinder fires.

A mysterious (and unknown until cleaning began) defect was this crack in 'CA' crankcase cover. First thoughts were that it was a result of some previous serious failure of the engine; crankcase penetration is not unusual in Deltic engines, although there was no sign of internal damage to any rotating parts within the engine.

It is reasonable to assume that the crack is as a result of the engine having been lowered onto the ground without suitable packing beneath the mountings and therefore resting on the crankcase cover at some point in its history.

Having got all three crankshafts out, attention turned to removing the pistons. There was now no little doubt that the engine seizure had been caused by pistons stuck in the cylinder bores, rather than by bearing failure or defect, or other unpleasant mechanical failure. If there was any doubt it was removed when the attempts were made to remove the pistons.

About two-thirds of the pistons were removed with relative ease but six or so were well and truly stuck. A period of two weeks followed with little progress while huge amounts of penetrating oil were unloaded into the cylinder bores containing the stuck pistons.

The success of the penetrating oil was limited; two pistons could be drawn out with some force but the remaining four needed attention from a substantial hardwood drift and copper hammer. Once they began to move, even the severely stuck pistons gave up the fight and were liberated.

The picture below is taken looking down the bore of B1 cylinder. Clearly visible are the inlet (closest to the camera) and exhaust ports in the cylinder liner, one of the drive shafts for the turbocharger is seen behind the forked big-end of C1 exhaust piston.

The pistons on a Deltic engine are a two-piece assembly comprising an aluminium body to which is attached a copper-alloy (Hidural) crown.

This arrangement is necessary because of the high exhaust temperatures generated in a two-stroke engine – unlike a four-stroke engine every stroke is a firing stroke and the pistons do not get any opportunity to cool. The thermal qualities of copper are more suited to this arrangement hence the use of a separate crown.

Two-piece pistons are not without their problems. Piston design would itself be a suitable subject for a whole book as it went through several iterations before a wholly suitable design was produced – this wasn't achieved until after the T9-29 engine came out of service. Even at the end of the service life of the D18-25B engines in Class 55 locomotives, pistons were still a major contributory factor in premature engine failure.

Fingers crossed, eh?

On display (below) in front of the main generator are the 18 pistons after removal.

The cleaning and inspection of the pistons and associated connecting rods, caps and bearings was to be the most laborious and time-consuming task of the whole project.

The full process comprised detergent soaking, low-pressure cold cleaning, more detergent soaking, high-pressure hot cleaning, petrol wash, chemical de-carbonising, petrol wash, hand cleaning of piston ring grooves, pressure test and non-destructive testing of connecting rods.

Of some surprise is that only one piston showed any signs of defect – A3 exhaust, which had a loose crown. By what can only be considered a minor miracle the project owned a spare, albeit of the Mk IV design – the others in the engine being Mk III. In a conventional engine the separation of connecting rod and piston is relatively simple, involving the removal of a circlip and pressing out a gudgeon pin. Deltics are not so.

The gudgeon pin (which connects the piston to the connecting rod) is contained in a gudgeon pin housing and is completely enclosed by the piston body - removal requires a specialist tool the manufacture of which was not feasible for a one-off requirement such as this.

Regarding the aforementioned minor miracle and the need for the specialist tool, one of the project members is employed (albeit in a different division) by the company now responsible for overhaul and repair of the Royal Navy Deltic engines – Rolls-Royce plc. Enquiries were made to see if they could help and the wheels of industry were set in motion.

After a nerve-racking couple of weeks while R-R considered the merits of assistance, they kindly agreed to help and the piston and con-rod assembly was on its way to Winsford to have the defective piston body removed and replaced by our spare.

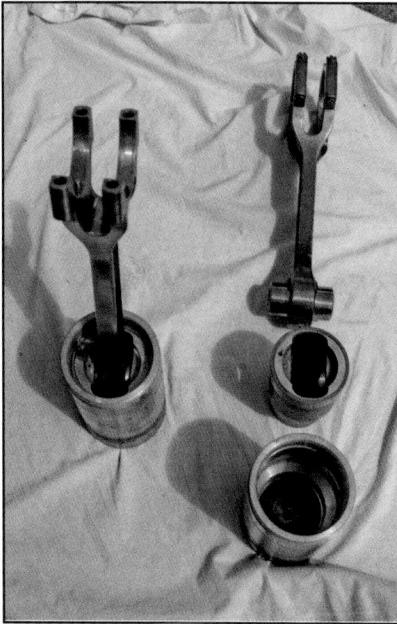

The defective piston (right) with its replacement (left). The 'forked' big end denotes an exhaust piston.

Pistons and connecting rods, before and after cleaning. The 'blade' big end denotes an inlet piston.

The refurbishment of the pistons and connecting rods was completed by the renewal of all the compression and oil-scraper rings, these being fitted just prior to the installation of the pistons.

18 pistons and connecting rods, complete with new compression and oil-scraper rings, sit ready for installation to the engine.

Chapter ten
Governor and fuel pumps

The governor, complete, with its bevel-drive gearbox and oil pump assembly was one of the more critical areas of the refurbishment. Deltic engines have a very low moment of inertia (i.e. they accelerate and decelerate extremely rapidly) as a result of having no flywheel. To control the engine at the required speed accurately the governor must work as designed at all times – failure to do so can lead to serious engine failure in a very short space of time.

The governor after refurbishment. Seen from bottom to top, the pneumatic hydraulic actuator, main governor body, (right) load control switches, speed demand and load control linkages, electrical connections to engine run solenoid, (top left) engine run solenoid cover.

The other side of the governor shows (bottom to top) governor oil pump, bevel-drive gearbox, output control link to fuel racks, maximum speed stop.

The governor clean and refurbishment was the same process as applied to the other components, and was completed with a rig test to ensure that the governor responded correctly to various speed demand and load simulation inputs.

This rig test gave us the confidence that the governor would actually control the engine when attempts were made to start it later.

Of equal criticality to the governor were the components which it directly controlled – the fuel injection pumps. These precision pumps (seen here on the right) – one for each cylinder – control the amount of fuel injected into the cylinder and therefore the engine speed. The relationship between these pumps and the governor is clear, as is the need for specialist overhaul.

The injection pumps and fuel injectors (one of which is seen on the left of this photograph) were sent to Colchester Fuel Injection Ltd, who (amongst their many other customers) repair and overhaul fuel injection equipment for the Royal Navy Deltics as a sub-contractor to Rolls-Royce.

Chapter eleven
VDA

As work with the engine progressed, it became more and more obvious that we could turn out an engine that would actually run. The idea that we could demonstrate the engine to enthusiasts and members of the public led to us successfully negotiating with the DPS to take possession of this VDA van which was surplus to their requirements.

It became the ideal facility for us. We were able to store spares and refurbished parts at one end, unrefurbished parts at the other end and build the engine in between. All the external doors opened individually and partitions were easily made from the removed wooden floor covering.

The most obvious advantage of the van was that there was now no need to build the engine on the shop floor and then find a means of transporting and lifting it to install it – everything easily went in on a fork-lift truck.

A section of the roof was removed to permit access into the van with a hoist and a section of the floor was removed to permit the installation of the bottom ('CA') crankshaft and pistons from below (outside) the van. Altogether the perfect solution; albeit a temporary one as detailed in chapter 14.

Chapter twelve
Rebuild

Once each of the many power unit components had been stripped, cleaned, inspected, repaired as required and tested, it was time for rebuilding and reassembly.

The first part of this mammoth task was to install the bare triangle in the VDA.

Sitting on its new mounts the triangle, bereft of virtually all moving parts, was trial fitted in early May 2008.

Facing the camera is the engine free end, with the three air manifold ducts, the three shaft driven gears for the turbocharger and free end gearbox and the hole mentioned in chapter 11 beneath the engine, clearly visible.

The garden hose coiled up on top of the engine was left on from the pressure test – it was used to create a 'head' of coolant in the absence of a header tank.

Prior to the installation of the sandwich piece all the internal coolant vent hoses were renewed.

For comparison the other end of the engine (the drive end) is seen here.

The taps on the ends of the three corrugated coolant hoses are another remnant of the pressure test and were removed prior to the refitting of the exhaust manifolds.

The spline drive arrangement for the camshafts (which, on a two-stroke engine only serve to operate the fuel injection pumps) can be seen leading out of 'BC' (upper left) crankcase and into 'B' bank cambox.

Along with the cylinder liners, the camboxes were just about the only components not removed from the engine.

The first major work undertaken as part of the rebuild was the installation of the piston and con-rod assemblies. This task, whilst not technically demanding, required a degree of skill owing to the need for a specific technique to ensure that no damage was caused to the (relatively soft) piston body by the (hard) cylinder liner as a result of poor alignment of the two items. Also, the piston was now fitted with new rings which were reluctant to slide easily along the inside of the special ring compressor used during insertion.

As with so many tasks on the project, use was made of tools lent freely by the DPS, a fine example of which was the piston ring compressor – an apparently simple but invaluable piece of equipment without which the installation of the pistons would not have been possible.

Above: Looking up into 'CA' crankcase after the installation of the 'A' bank exhaust pistons. These pistons are fitted from above, through 'AB' crankcase.

Below: And again into 'CA' crankcase, this time after all 'A' exhaust and 'C' inlet pistons have been installed.

With all 18 pistons installed and pushed well into the cylinders out of the way, the crankshafts could be fitted. This is 'AB' crankcase, now complete with crankshaft and main bearing caps. The gear just visible on the left-hand end of the crankshaft drives one of the shafts to the turbocharger and the spline drive to 'A' bank camshaft.

Inserted in the drive end (left-hand in the photograph) is the tool for turning the crankshaft as required during the rebuild, this is hard work – certainly with any precision – as the new rings fitted to the pistons develop significant friction within the cylinder liners. As described in chapter 9, for dismantling and reassembly it is desirable to turn the crankshafts to a convenient position to allow relatively easy access to the big end nuts. Now, with the engine free, this was a luxury previously unknown.

The process is repeated for the other two crankshafts, with again 'CA' being by far and away the most difficult due the action of gravity trying to force the crankshaft into your face at all times. The installation of 'CA' crankshaft was undertaken by supporting it on its cleaning / transport stand and lowering the engine down on to it from a hoist above. It was then held in place using a system of wooden blocks and lever whilst the main bearing caps were secured, it's not the kind of job you'd want to do daily.

With the three crankshafts installed the phasing case could be refitted. There are 126 studs, nuts and washers holding the phasing case to the engine – most of them in extremely awkward positions. As a consequence the fitting took two of us six hours to complete.

The phasing case is seen above having just been reunited with the engine. Covered by a sheet to its left is the main generator and similarly covered to the right of the engine is the turbocharger. Note the use of wooden blanks on the fuel injector and exhaust manifold mounts, also the temporary fitment of the crankcase covers, this to prevent ingress of foreign objects.

Still to be fitted to the phasing case at this stage is its output flange to the generator – this will go where the rag is in the centre of the case.

With the three crankshafts and the phasing case fitted the engine could now be timed ('phased' to use the Napier nomenclature). This is a lengthy procedure where all the crankshafts' angular positions are set relative to each other before each camshaft is set relative to its driving crankshaft.

The photograph on the next page shows the method used to set the initial phasing position.

The dial on the left records the angular position of the crankshaft; the dial test indicator is held in place by Heath-Robinson and shows the longitudinal position of the connecting rod, and therefore the piston. The phasing process uses 'C1' exhaust piston as the datum. 'BC' crankshaft is therefore the first one to have the phasing set.

The whole procedure is as follows; a tool (comprising a battery, cables, an electric contact and an indicator lamp) to determine the position of the piston is inserted through the fuel injector pocket and fixed in position, the engine is hand-turned in the normal direction of rotation until the lamp lights.

The angular position of 'BC' crankshaft is recorded and the engine turned again in the normal direction until the lamp extinguishes and the position of 'BC' crankshaft is recorded again. Because the lamp is lit only when the contact on the position tool is in contact with the piston crown, the angular position halfway between the lamp on and lamp off points must therefore be 'top dead centre' (TDC) of the piston. This point is then marked on the crankshaft position dial and the crankshaft rotated through almost one full turn and stopped at TDC.

The piston position indicator is then moved and fixed as above to record the position of 'B1' exhaust piston, which is now also set to TDC. With the quillshaft between 'AB' crankshaft and the phasing case temporarily withdrawn so as not to rotate the crankshaft, the engine is hand turned until the angular position dial on 'BC' crankshaft shows 40° after TDC (this being the phase angle between the cylinder banks). 'AB' quillshaft can now be re-engaged and two of the three crankshafts are phased.

With the TDC tool moved to 'A1' exhaust piston, the process is repeated, this time setting 'BC' crankshaft to read 80° after TDC with 'A1' exhaust piston at TDC.

The whole process is then repeated, this time without withdrawing the quillshafts, and the TDC position of 'C1', 'B1' and 'A1' pistons is checked against 'BC' crankshaft position to an accuracy of +/- ¼°.

The photo above shows the piston position indicator, with the lamp lit, while fitted to 'B1' cylinder.

Having set the phasing of all three crankshafts relative to each other, the camshafts are set, this time using the helpfully-provided-by-Napier graduated scale on the end of each camshaft. This scale is seen through an aperture covered by the square four-hole plate in the top right of the photograph above.

With no valve gear to worry about, the sole-purpose of the camshaft is to operate the fuel injection pumps. The angular position of the camshaft sets the point at which fuel injection commences and its accurate setting is therefore just as important as crankshaft phasing.

The datum for setting the camshafts is set by the relationship to the no. 1 exhaust piston for whatever bank is being set. The datum varies between engine types, but, for the T9-29 engine the commencement of injection point is 27° before TDC.

The free-end gearbox was next in line for installation, a reasonably simple task made even easier as it was built and fitted by a project member who maintains a Supermarine Spitfire for a living.

The free end gearbox casing already in position, the upper gear is the drive from the opposite end of the engine, taken off 'CA' crankshaft.

And seen again with the end cover in place.

The date was mid-September 2008 by now, and we were pressing ahead to try to get the engine to a state where it could be started at the upcoming DPS (FP commemoration) open day in October. This was to be a massive (and, in the event, fruitless) effort by all project members, the calendar beating us to it.

The next assembly to be fitted was the main generator. As noted in a previous chapter this machine weighs almost as much as the engine itself and its installation required the use of a hired-in crane.

A flange mounted machine such as this requires some degree of skill to fit. The entire assembly needs to be aligned accurately to allow the bolts securing it to the engine and the bolts securing its adapter ring to be fitted.

Photo: Ian Lewis

The main generator, with the auxiliary generator now mounted on top of it, is seen shortly after being fitted to the engine. The adapter ring between the generator and the engine is in two pieces, only the bottom piece had been installed at the time of this photograph. Unseen here is the generator cooling fan (also a two-piece affair) which has to be installed after the flange mounting is secured; there is just enough space to fit each half of the fan between the armature shaft and the inner edge of the adapter ring.

The alignment and fitting of the fan took nearly as long again as the whole generator installation did.

The G-cramp method of securing the generator to its mounting pedestal and the non-horizontal alignment of the power unit were both temporary. The pedestals were borrowed from the DPS whilst we waited for delivery of our purpose made ones. The G-cramps provided more than enough restraint for the short shunt of the VDA between the location where the lift took place and the DPS Depot.

The sandwich piece is the adaptor between the free end of the triangle and whatever intake air charging device is installed – dependent on the engine type and application.

It also forms part of the coolant system and requires an air tight seal for the intake air.

So, with the internal coolant vent hoses renewed, 'Hermetite' jointing compound was applied to the scrupulously clean mating surfaces on the engine ready for the installation of the sandwich piece.

Note that the turbocharger drive gears have been temporarily removed, to be refitted once the sandwich piece is installed. An oil seal is made by a rubber interface around the outer edge of the gear bearing housing.

A couple of hours later, and with the turbocharger drive gears now refitted and locked into position, the sandwich piece installation is complete.

Note the hand-written cylinder bank identification on 'B' bank and the crankcases – also the indication of normal direction of rotation of the crankshaft.

This was done to ensure that there was little chance of error when phasing the engine earlier in the week.

I realise that this sounds ridiculous, but, three crankshafts one rotating in a different direction to the other two, ¼ degree of accuracy required – the risks needed mitigation. Many were the times we asked each other "are you sure?" before moving on to the next stage of timing.

The photograph on page 65 demonstrates the result of attention to detail.

In what was a day of solid achievements, the turbocharger was installed just over three hours later (above).

A critical part of the installation of the turbo is the correct meshing of the driving and driven gears. This is observed through inspection covers which are just visible on the photograph (above) on either side of the turbo. With the gears engaged it is necessary to attempt to turn the engine by the use of a torque wrench on the turbocharger turbine and record the torque applied when the second of the two drive gears begins to turn. Failure to observe this correctly could mean a disproportionate load being applied to one of the gears with premature failure of the drive being the inevitable result.

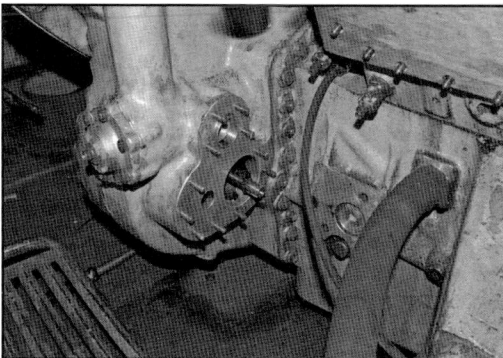

The pressure and scavenge oil pumps were installed next. Seen here is the mount for the pressure pump, complete with the drive shaft already in place. The nipple to the left of the mount is the oil pressure gauge (and switch) connection.

Like so many components there is no wasted space around the pumps and installation provided a particular challenge, with more than enough of the securing nuts being out of easy reach – even with long thin fingers. As the rebuild stage of the project neared completion, the components which were more vulnerable to damage could be installed.

The governor is seen here newly assembled to the phasing case. The governor controls the engine speed, and via a series of feedback linkages, two switches and the main generator field, the engine load. The trailing lead and plug provides the connection to the locomotive engine run and stop circuits.

The arm on the right of the governor is the output lever which directly controls the fuel racks, and therefore, engine speed. The label behind the governor reads 'ring nut to secure', this refers to the back of the shaft which drives the auxiliary generator and is hidden once the overspeed trip device is fitted.

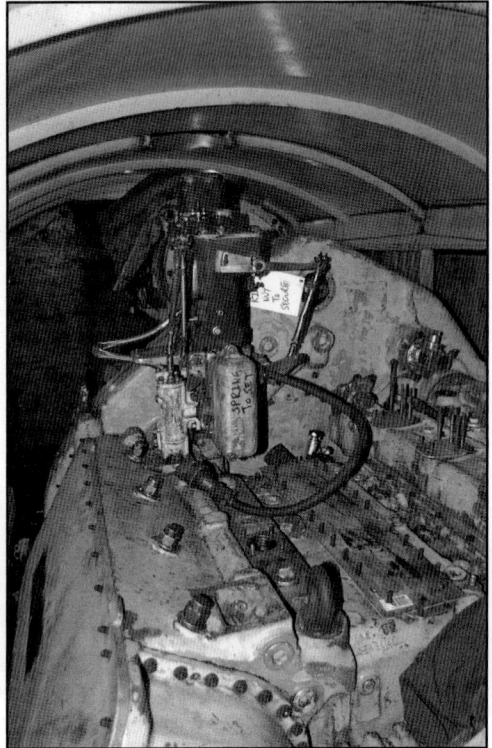

On the next page the governor and its relationship with the control linkage is seen in an extract from the Napier Training Notes. The overspeed trip device (5) is connected to the overspeed governor (12). The overspeed governor is driven off a shaft from the phasing case and senses (by centrifugal force acting on a number of rotating flyweights) the speed of the engine. When the engine speed rises above the 'trip' speed the force on the flyweights is sufficient to move the operating lever within the governor which in turn causes the lever connected to the trip cylinder to unlatch a pawl. This action releases a spring pack, which through connected linkages overcomes and closes the fuel racks regardless of the position set by the engine governor, to stop the engine. This arrangement protects the engine (and the main generator) against overspeed caused by governing fault or extreme and sudden unloading.

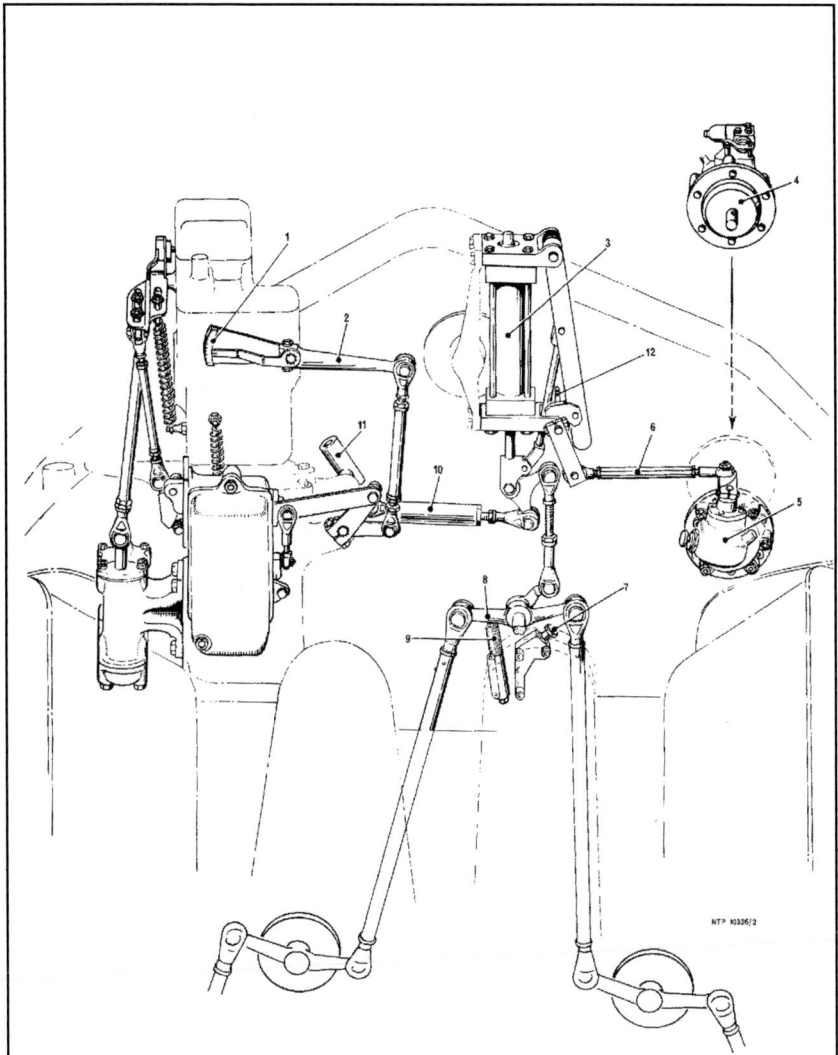

FIG. 1 LAYOUT OF CONTROLS

1. Governor output scale
2. Governor output lever
3. Overspeed trip unit
4. Underspeed governor
5. Overspeed governor
6. Overspeed governor link
7. Maximum stop
8. Double lever
9. Minimum stop
10. Overload spring link
11. Adjustable lever
12. Tripping lever

(Above) Three overhauled fuel injection pumps, still with their plastic protective covers fitted over the delivery union, gleam just after installation to 'A' cylinder bank.

The control rod from the engine governor will be connected to the lever at the far left of the photograph. This lever acts upon a shaft which turns the racks, connecting all the pumps together. These racks act on a worm gear within the pump which, as it rotates under the control of the rack, rotates a helix to control the amount of fuel being injected into the cylinder. The amount of fuel injected is proportional to the load on, and speed of, the engine.

See the appendix at the rear of this book for a description of engine and load control.

Above the injection pumps is the inlet manifold (more usually referred to as the air manifold) and below them is the exhaust manifold.

The shaft to the left of the air manifold is the spline drive from 'AB' crankcase gears to 'A' bank camshaft.

The pipe in front of the exhaust manifold is the (yet to be renewed in this photograph) oil drain from the 'A' bank cambox to 'CA' crankcase.

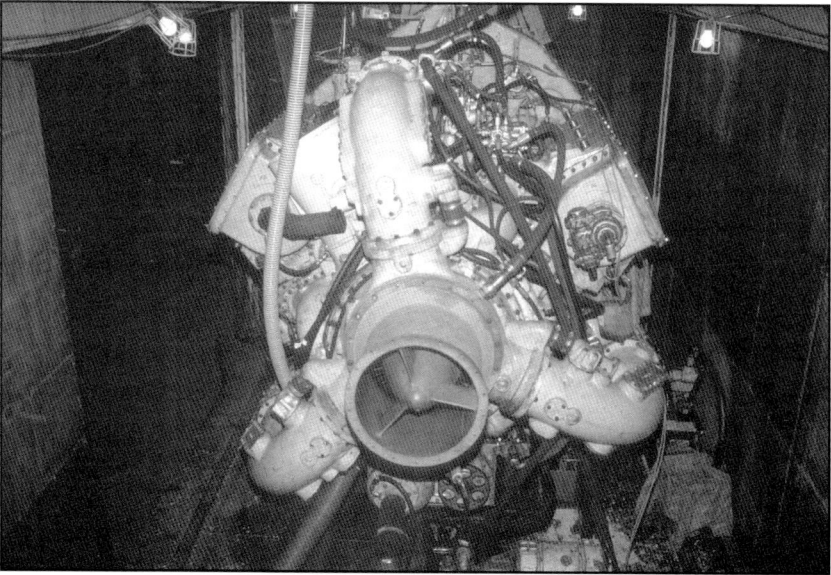

Photo: Richard Senior

The engine, now complete and ready for priming, is seen above in October 2008. The hose going vertically is the make-up connection to the header tank, which ensures that the engine is always full of coolant and allows for expansion and contraction of the coolant contents as the engine heats, and cools.

The other hose going to the roof is the coolant vent to the header tank, this connects all the individual vent hoses around the engine, via a venting vessel mounted on 'B' bank exhaust manifold, to the header tank and ensures that any air in the coolant system is allowed to escape to atmosphere and doesn't cause any air locks.

The large bore hose at the bottom of the photograph is the coolant loop from the engine outlet to the pump inlet; this is taking (temporary) place of the cooler group which was not yet sourced.

Chapter thirteen
Preparations for initial running

We had completed the renovation of the power unit in slightly over 18-months, with the exception of the fuel injection equipment and piston body change it was all done with volunteer labour. The final tasks were on the ancillary components necessary to provide services when the engine was running.

The engine is started by connecting the main generator across a battery and the generator's internal starting field (i.e. 'motoring' the engine). The battery used for this was kindly loaned by the DPS, being surplus to their requirements at the time.

To control the switching of the battery for starting the engine, two start contactors are used.

These need to be robust in order to handle the (potentially) very large currents present during starting, as do the cables which connect the battery to the generator – these have a cross-sectional area of 60 sq mm – compared to average domestic wiring of between 1.5 to 4 sq mm.

The support arrangement seen in this picture is very temporary in this state, only being used for the first start before a more permanent mounting was built.

The fuel is raised from the (temporary) tank through a filter (seen behind the pump) and to the distribution and pressurising assembly by this electric pump.

Note its circuit breaker, cable strapped to the oil return pipe, just in case.

Photo: Richard Senior

With all of the services built and connected it was time to 'prove the pudding' by attempting to start the engine. Pressure gauges were fitted to the main oil gallery and fuel distributor and the systems primed and checked, the coolant system was filled and checked for leaks and the electrical controls were tested and re-tested – specifically to ensure that a demand for the engine to stop was met with the appropriate governor response – i.e. to set the fuel racks to the 'no fuel' position.

The engine had been spun over as if for starting several times previously, for testing purposes and for demonstration at the DPS Finsbury Park gala, but on this occasion there was greater tension in the air – this time it was for real.

In order to be absolutely certain that the engine was under our control and could not run away as a result of a governing or fuelling fault we had taken two additional precautions prior to any start attempts. The first was to place a choke plate across the air intake duct; this would greatly restrict the flow of air available for combustion and therefore inhibit any tendency for the engine to self-destruct through overspeeding. The second was to affix a pull-cord to the trip mechanism of the overspeed device. This could be manually operated in the event of anything untoward occurring and would result in the closure of the fuel racks, and thus an engine stop, regardless of any other control input – demanded or otherwise.

So, on 22 October, with one person on the start control circuit breaker, one on the overspeed trip and one watching the oil pressure, we were ready. The plan was first to spin the engine without allowing the engine governor to open the fuel racks, then check for leaks and other difficulties – this went off without issue.

For the next attempt the fuel lift pump was started and the fuel pressure rose in the fuel galleries. The engine was spun again and the governor engine run solenoid was energised. The engine spun and after about 20 seconds the output lever on the governor moved under the influence of oil pressure and the fuel racks opened – then there was smoke, exhaust smoke.

As soon as the smoke was seen the engine was stopped (at this stage it was enough simply to open the start control circuit breaker) and a cursory inspection was made all around the engine.

A further attempt was undertaken, this time the intention was that if the engine started the engine run solenoid would immediately be de-energised to ensure that the fuel racks closed and the engine would stop when demanded – this passed without difficulty.

So now, after all the checking and all the testing we elected to start the engine and let it run. Oil primed, fuel pump on, start circuit energised – engine motoring, engine run solenoid energised – fuel racks opened up, smoke – pure white smoke from unburnt diesel, then, with the exhaust note now rapidly increasing in pitch and frequency, it ran.

I'll write that again, it ran – for the first time in over 30-years the sole-remaining T9-29 engine was running again, restored from a seized lump to a running engine. It was a superb achievement – with a project of this magnitude there is always doubt right up to the point where the engine runs. However hard you try and whatever precautions you take there is always the chance that Murphy's Law will apply. The description of the start above has been compressed a little so as not to bore the reader but it was, I think it's fair to say, a good day's work.

Before we could all retire for the night in celebration the engineering tasks continued a little longer. Here the crankcase cover has been removed to expose 'BC' crankshaft to permit an inspection of the bearings and other components after the short run. This was to be repeated after each of the initial runs. *(Ian Lewis)*

The photo below shows the engine running on one of the subsequent starts. The haze is exhaust gas; as the picture on the previous page demonstrates, there was no exhaust system fitted other than the short stub attached to the turbocharger. The removable roof on the VDA wasn't removed at the time of the run, hence the cloud.

Photo: Ian Lewis

The first short runs had shown up some minor non-conformances;

- A coolant leak on a temporary tee-piece for the fill and drain connection, another on an adapter external to the engine and another on a blanking plate on 'C' bank exhaust.
- A fuel leak on a return-flow hose from 'C' cambox to the distributor assembly.
- Lubricating oil pressure was a little high.
- Idle speed was a little low.

The coolant and fuel leaks were easily cured, the oil pressure remains to be fully investigated – although high pressure is a far more desirable 'fault' than low pressure.

The idle speed was adjusted after a thorough check of the governor and fuel rack settings, both individually and in relation to each other. The relationship between the governor and the fuel rack is critical and requires a deep understanding of the system as a whole. Get it wrong in a minor way and you might lose a few hundred horsepower; get it wrong in a major way and the engine will run out of control to its inevitable demise.

We knew from the outset of the project that if we were to run the engine for any length of time we would need a cooler group[1] above almost anything else. For the initial engine runs a hose was taken from the engine coolant outlet connection and back into the coolant pump – this arrangement effectively replicated the set up on a locomotive up to the point where the coolant temperature rises to operate the by-pass valve[2]. This gave us around five minutes run time. A couple of attempts had been made to buy cooler groups from various sources – including ex-Class 43 (HST) refurbishment – but either the price was wrong or it became too difficult for the seller.

In the end, and with the benefit of hindsight, the solution was obvious – buy a locomotive.

---

(1) A cooler group is the modern vernacular for a radiator (or bank of radiators), a cooling fan and the associated pipework, by-pass valves and controls.
(2) The by-pass valve is the equivalent of a thermostat on a car, except that a car thermostat usually opens as a result of rising temperature to allow coolant through the radiator and a by-pass valve closes to prevent the by-pass of the radiator by the coolant.

Chapter fourteen

Loco

We had dimly entertained fantasies of loco conversion previously, though none of the tentative enquiries or purchase options had borne fruit.

It was only when 37372 was being stripped for spares by (Barrow Hill neighbours) HNRC prior to disposal that a real chance was presented. In the end the negotiations were engaged, took place and terminated in the car park at Barrow Hill in the space of around two minutes. I knew how much I could spend and this was tendered – and accepted.

Almost immediately, and once the Class 37 power unit was removed the BDP took possession of the loco.

The first task on the loco was to assess the options for installing the Deltic engine. It wasn't a case of ascertaining whether or not it would fit, rather, the best way to fit it.

Deltic engines are considerably smaller than their 4-stroke counterparts anyway but this one, with only 1100 bhp against the 1750 bhp of the Class 37 power unit just removed, was tiny – and light.

The photograph on the left is of the engine room prior to cleaning, an unpleasant process but necessary nonetheless. After the clean we were able to take detailed measurements (in all three planes), including the changes in loco centre of gravity.

With the loco engine room drawn up the design of the mountings could start.

The design process was followed quickly by manufacture of the mountings.

With the new mountings placed in position for a trial fit (photograph right), 37372's engine room nears the point where the Deltic engine could be lowered in.

From front to rear; the new generator end mounts (with a spirit level in place to prove horizontal alignment) sit on a new cross-member which itself picks up on the original Class 37 generator mounts; the new engine end mounts sit directly on the longitudinal 'I'- sections of the loco main frame; the (now redundant) Class 37 engine end mounts.

The prime reason for the acquisition of a loco is ably demonstrated in the two photographs on this page. Everything that we were struggling to get hold of in

Both photos: Richard Senior

order to make an operable demonstration engine a realistic proposition is contained in one place. Cooler group (and associated auxiliaries), control cubicle, load control resistors and auxiliary voltage control, air supply and a fuel tank - all in a nicely shaped vehicle.

Only six weeks after taking charge of the loco we were ready to install the engine. The photograph on the inside front cover shows the power unit about to be moved into position above the loco and some five or so minutes later, seen below, the engine is being lowered into 37372.

Photo: Gary Sidebottom

The new mountings within the loco body had been deliberately left unsecured to allow for realignment if required, but – apart from a small movement at the generator end - the positioning was spot on.

After final checks that all the bolt holes lined up, that the power unit was centred laterally and in the correct location longitudinally the unit was secured and the crane detached. The loco roof was dropped into place and the task was complete – the whole process took little more than 90 minutes.

The photograph above represents a real landmark in the project's work to date. Seen from no. 2 end of the engine room looking towards no. 1 end the power unit sits in its new home.

The cables suspended from the roof in the photograph at the bottom of page 69 are the power cables from the main generator into the control cubicle. They connect to the generator terminal bars (the enclosure for one of which is just visible at the bottom of the photograph above) on either side of the machine, one side is positive, the other negative.

To say that the installation was done 'on paper' alone up until the point that the power unit was lowered in, the fit is remarkable. The locomotive cables all fit without any length alterations, the power unit is absolutely dead centre longitudinally and laterally and spot on the centre of gravity in all three planes. The unit doesn't foul any of the cross-members in the locomotive bedplate and the height of the locomotive roof is more than sufficient to allow headroom clearance between it and the top of the governor – the unit's highest point.

As mentioned elsewhere, Deltic engines are 'dry-sump' and require a separate oil tank to supply the lubrication system, it was therefore necessary to install the tank used temporarily in the VDA to 37372.

Modifications were also required to adapt the Class 37 coolant, fuel and oil priming systems to suit the Deltic engine. We have taken the opportunity to retain the electric oil priming pump fitted as standard on a Class 37 and use it for oil priming on our engine – Deltic locomotives are not fitted with electric pumps and priming can be a physical challenge with cold oil, why make life hard?

Seen on the photograph below (left to right) is the oil tank, fuel supply pipe, coolant vent pipe and the new exhaust system; note the absence of an exhaust silencer, we like our Napiers loud!

Chapter fifteen
The Baby Deltic Project

The story of how the power unit was discovered is told in chapter one and with the purchase of the power unit the project was formed. Our initial aim was simply to prevent our new asset deteriorating further and this was achieved as described by storage at MAN BW, then the DPS Depot. Subsequent to this aim there were only ideas and thoughts, until I left the DPS Board in 2006 – after a rest from Deltics the Baby Deltic Project was born and work commenced in earnest to see what I had bought.

Any club, society, or even company is only successful if the members can be united towards a common, realistic, goal. This project has achieved so much because the goal was never in doubt, neither was the desire. The BDP is also small, comprising only six members all of whom give generously of their time and money for no reason other than to see the project succeed. The fact that we have achieved so much despite the fact that most of the Project members have other, higher priority, demands on their time is testament to them, and this book is dedicated to;

Nigel Paine

Richard Wardle (front)

Richard Senior

Ian Lewis

Gary Sidebottom

Appendix one
Deltic engine description and Leading Technical Details

The Deltic is a compression ignition, two-stroke cycle, uniflow, triangular form, lightweight engine with opposed pistons and piston controlled ports for inlet and exhaust timing. It was developed by D. Napier & Son (from a Junkers pre-WWII design) to fulfil a post-WWII Admiralty propulsion requirement for torpedo boats.

Referring to figures one and two on the following pages and considering one cylinder in isolation, the basic principle of operation is as follows;

- The cylinder contains two pistons which are connected at the big-end to a crankshaft.

- Each piston controls the uncovering and covering of its relevant port (be-it inlet or exhaust).

- The exhaust piston 'leads' the inlet piston by 20° of crankshaft rotation, the exhaust piston covers the exhaust port before the inlet piston covers the inlet port and a small degree of pressure charging of the cylinder occurs as a result.

- As the pistons come together, and after the inlet port is covered the air trapped in the cylinder is compressed and its temperature rises rapidly.

- At a point (varying between engine types) about 30° before the exhaust piston reaches top dead centre (i.e. the limit of its stroke) fuel injection commences.

- The fuel injected into the cylinders burns immediately and creates a massive pressure rise which forces the pistons apart.

- Combustion is complete by the time the exhaust piston uncovers the exhaust port and allows spent gases to pass to atmosphere.

- Once the inlet piston has uncovered the inlet port intake air is free to pass through the cylinder from the inlet to the exhaust port (i.e. uniflow). This both cools and scavenges the cylinder prior to the cycle repeating.

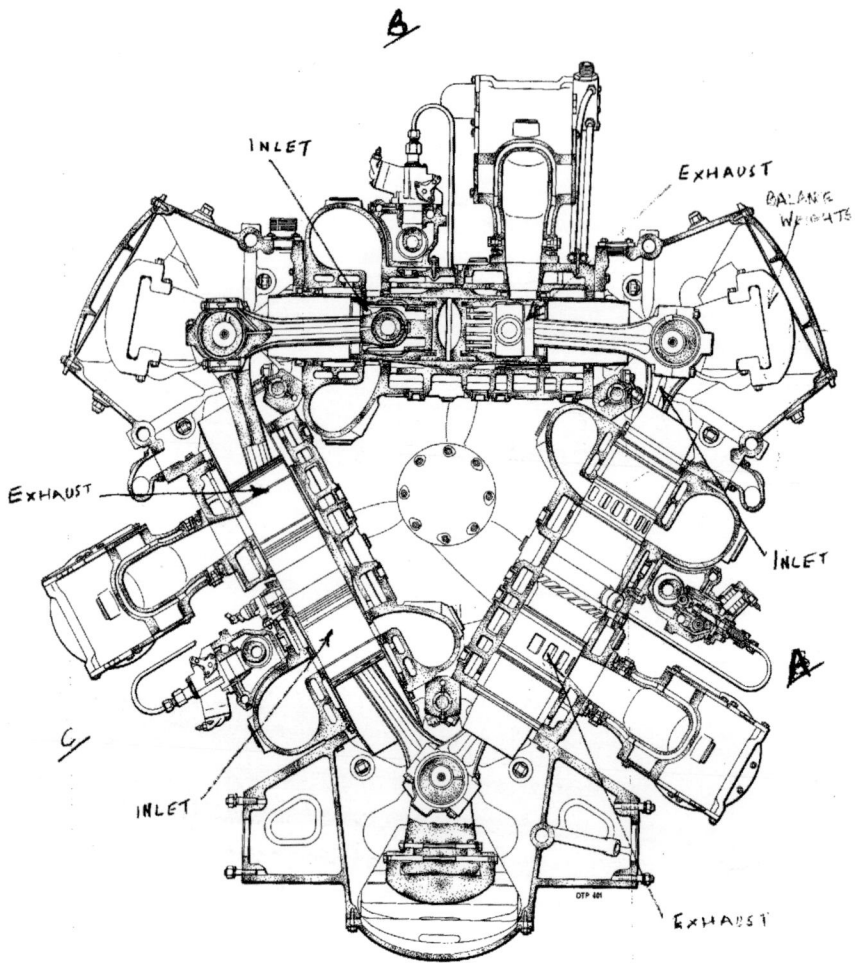

B

INLET

EXHAUST

BALANCE
WEIGHTS

EXHAUST

INLET

EXHAUST

C

INLET

B

VIEW FROM GENERATOR END

DTP 401

FIG. 1   DELTIC ENGINE, TYPE T9-29
CROSS SECTION THROUGH No. 2 CYLINDERS

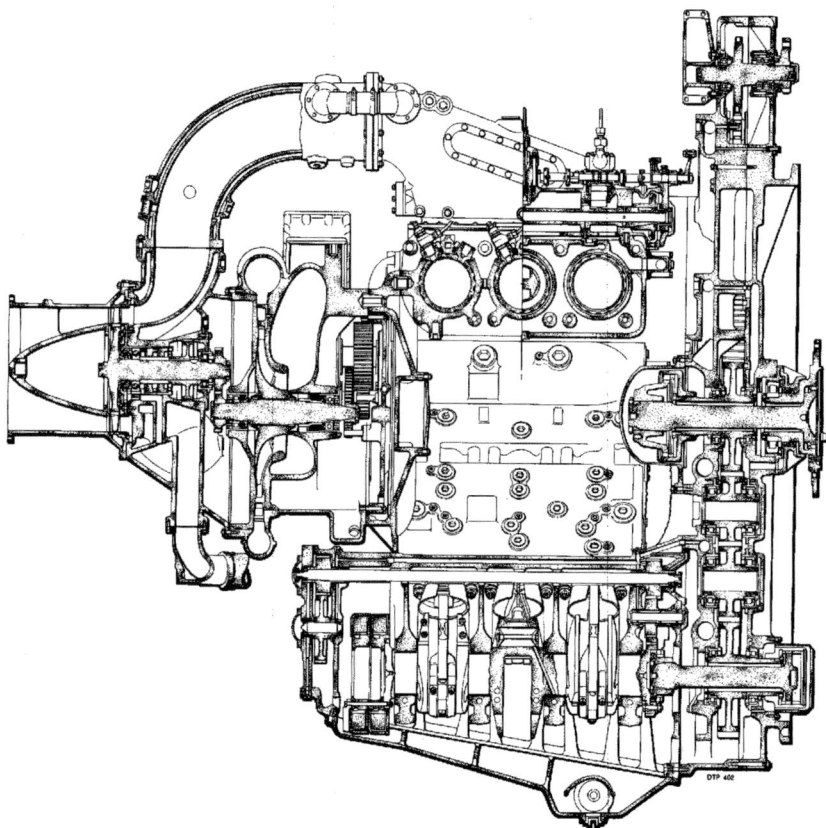

FIG. 2 DELTIC ENGINE, TYPE T9-29
LONGITUDINAL SECTION THROUGH ENGINE

Two-stroke, port controlled engines are reluctant to start because of the lack of a large induction stroke and the consequent lack of sufficient vacuum to draw air into the cylinder before the compression stroke. This is mitigated by the use of an engine-driven pressure charger to force air for combustion into the cylinder whilst it is being turned (relatively) slowly for starting. Deltics have either a scavenge-blower or a turbo-blower, depending on engine type.

Class 55 locos have type D18-25B engines with scavenge-blowers, these employ purely engine driven turbines to create inlet pressure.

Referring to figure two, the Project's engine, type T9-29, has an engine driven turbocharger which employs a similar arrangement to the '25B' until the engine revs rise and power increases, exhaust gasses then act on a driving turbine within the turbocharger which relieves the load on the engine driven gears.

Figure 3. Identification of cylinders within the engine.

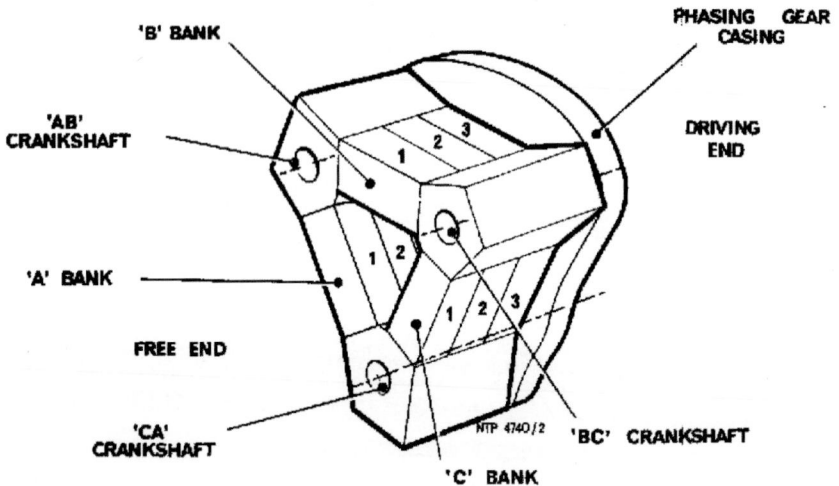

Figure 4. The relationship between the pistons relative to each other, and the firing order of the complete engine.

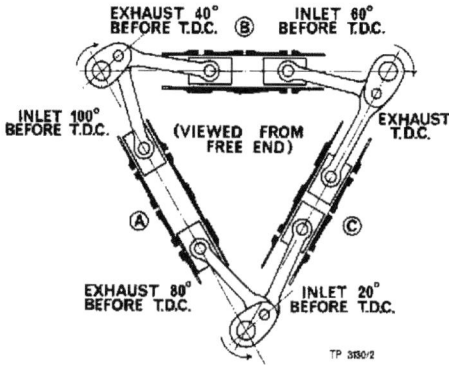

EXHAUST 40°
BEFORE T.D.C. Ⓑ INLET 60°
BEFORE T.D.C.

INLET 100°
BEFORE T.D.C.

(VIEWED FROM
FREE END)

EXHAUST
T.D.C.

Ⓐ

Ⓒ

EXHAUST 80°
BEFORE T.D.C.

INLET 20°
BEFORE T.D.C.

TP 3130/2

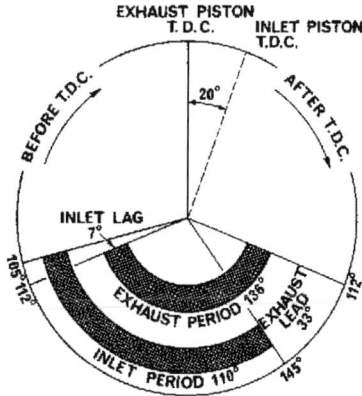

EXHAUST PISTON
T.D.C.

INLET PISTON
T.D.C.

20°

BEFORE T.D.C.

AFTER T.D.C.

INLET LAG
7°

105° 112°

EXHAUST PERIOD 136°

EXHAUST LEAD 33°

112°

INLET PERIOD 110°

145°

NTP 4731/2

CYL. BANK	MEAN CRANK ANGLE (C.1, CYLINDER) — DEGREES														
	0	25	50	75	100	125	150	175	200	225	250	275	300	325	350
C	1				3					2					
B		1					3				2				
A			1					3				2			

NTP 4730/1

79

Extract from Napier Training Notes

ENGINE

Type	T9-29
Description	Opposed-piston, liquid-cooled, two-stroke, turbo-blown, compression-ignition engine
Number of cylinders	Nine
Arrangement	Three banks of three cylinders forming a triangular configuration
Overall dimensions	Length 86.25 in (2191 mm) Width 71 in (1805 mm) Height 90.25 in (2292 mm)
Bore	5.125 in (130.2 mm)
Stroke	7.25 in x 2 (184.14 mm x 2)
Swept volume	2,692 cu.in (44.15 litres) total
Compression ratio	20.7:1 nominal 16.0:1 effective
Expansion ratio	14.0:1
Rated output (B.S.649-1949)	1100 b.h.p. (1115 metric h.p.) at 1600 crankshaft r.p.m.
B.M.E.P. at rated output	101 lb/sq.in. (7.90 kg/cm^2)
Piston speed at 1600 crankshaft r.p.m.	1932 ft/min (5888 cm/min)

TURBO BLOWER

Type - turbine	Triple-entry, single-stage
blower	Single-stage, single-speed, single-entry, centrifugal
Turbine wheel	12.875 in (327.025 mm) diameter
Impeller	15.5 in (393.7 mm) diameter single-sided
Pressure (blower)	12.9 lb/sq.in. (0.907 kg/cm^2) (gauge) at rated output
Gear ratio (turbine)	1.161:1 blower/turbine
(blower)	9.006:1 engine/blower

Extract from Napier Training Notes

INJECTION TIMING

Timing Variable

Datum setting: 27° before exhaust T.D.C. with the control shafts at maximum.

Camshaft casing setting pin datum

124°

Injection pumps control shaft setting (at 0° governor output scale setting)

96°

FUEL

FUEL

Specification

Diesel fuel to BS 2869 Class A

Specific gravity

0.830 at 60°F $(15.6^{\circ}$C$)$

Net calorific value

18,500 B.Th.u.(10,280 kcal/kg)

FUEL SYSTEM

Circulating pressure

20 lb/sq.in. $(1.406$ kg/cm$^2)$

Injection pumps

Napier/C.A.V. type FM 110 B5, one per cylinder

Injectors

One C.A.V. nozzle type BDL 15 6230 per cylinder

LUBRICATING OIL

Specification

(see Section 28)

Main Pressure

80 lb/sq.in $(5.62$ kg/cm$^2)$ nominal (1600 crankshaft r.p.m.)

Shut-down pressure

20 lb/sq.in $(1.4$ kg/cm$^2)$

OIL CONSUMPTION

At rated power

4.5 Imperial pt/hr (2.56 litres/hr)

GREASES

Controls, governor switch linkage Radiator fan shafts and couplings

(see Section 28)

Extract from Napier Training Notes

COOLING

ENGINE COOLING

Type   Closed coolant circuit with air cooled radiators.

Coolant   An anti-freeze coolant in the proportion 30 parts of inhibited ethylene glycol (see Section 28) to 70 parts by volume of distilled or chloride free, soft or artificially softened water.

Coolant differential pressure switch	Operating pressure 2 lb/sq.in.
High temperature warning switch	Operating temperature 195°F (90.6°C)
High temperature shut-down switch	Operating temperature 205°F (96.1°C)
Oil cooling	Air cooled radiators

TEMPERATURES

Nominal coolant outlet (at 1600 crankshaft r.p.m.)	185°F (85°C)
Maximum oil inlet	150°F (65°C)

SPEEDS AND ROTATIONS
(Viewed from free-end)

CRANKSHAFT

'AB' and 'BC' clockwise
'CA' anti-clockwise

AUXILIARY GENERATOR DRIVE

Output (included in rated b.h.p.)   Up to 90 h.p. at 2685 r.p.m. at 1600 crankshaft r.p.m.

Rotation   Clockwise

FANS DRIVE

Output (included in rated b.h.p.)   Anti-clockwise

Appendix two
Governor function and load control

A fundamental part of any engine is the means to control it. Any control system must;

- Allow the engine to be started.
- Allow the engine to idle ('tick-over').
- Control the engine speed between pre-determined limits.
- Intervene if such pre-determined limits are exceeded.
- Control the load on the engine.
- Stop the engine.

All of the above functions are satisfied by the governor and overspeed device.

The governor is mounted on the engine side of the phasing case, it comprises the following units which are considered as one assembly for ease of description;

- Bevel drive gearbox.
- Oil pump.
- Load control switch box.
- Speed setting (input, or demand function) linkage.
- Fuel rack setting (output function) linkage.

Referring to figure five - a schematic diagram of the governor, engine oil is drawn from the phasing case gallery and pumped by the governor oil pump round the governor, this oil serves both to lubricate the governor and provide its control medium.

Consider the governor when the engine is being motored for starting. An electrically controlled valve (the engine run solenoid (1)) is opened under the control of the loco electrical circuits to allow oil to flow to the governor shut-down valve (19). This valve opens and in turn allows oil to flow (via the main pilot valve (16)) to the underside of the power piston (13), overcoming the action of the power piston return spring and causing it to rise. The power piston acts on a crank which rotates about the output shaft (12) and moves the fuel rack in the 'increase fuel' direction.

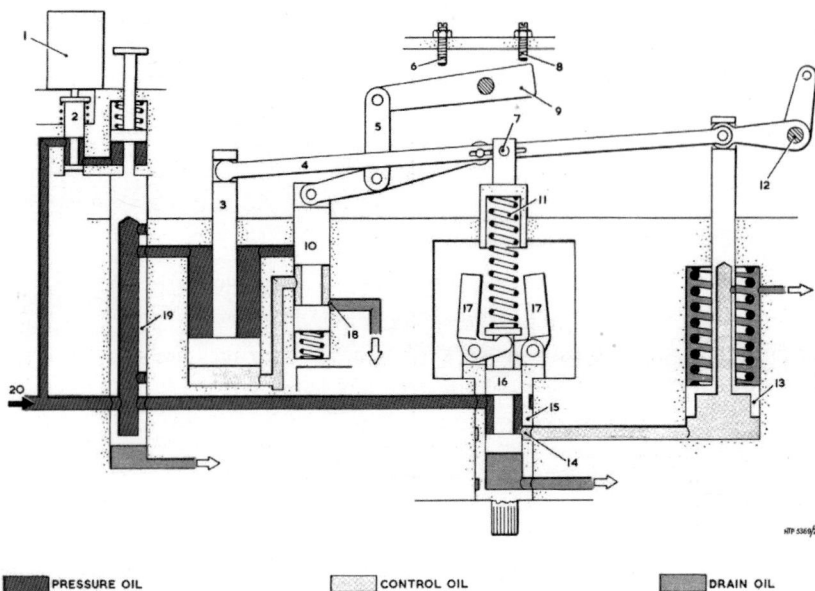

PRESSURE OIL	CONTROL OIL	DRAIN OIL

1. Shut-down solenoid
2. Solenoid valve
3. Speed re-set piston
4. Floating lever
5. Forked lever
6. Idling speed stop screw
7. Trunnion
8. Maximum speed stop screw
9. Speed-control shaft
10. Speed re-set valve
11. Speeder spring
12. Output shaft
13. Power piston
14. Power piston regulating port
15. Flyweight sleeve
16. Main pilot valve
17. Flyweights
18. Speed re-set valve regulating port
19. Shut-down valve
20. Inlet

Figure 5. Governor functioning, schematic drawing.

The speed sensing flyweights (17) are connected to the bevel gearbox which in turn is connected to a gear within the phasing case – the rotational speed of the flyweights is therefore directly related to engine speed. As the engine fires and the revs begin to increase, the speed sensing section of the governor comes into play. The flyweights (17) move out under the influence of centrifugal force, this causes the main pilot valve (16) to lift and allow oil to drain from the underside of the power piston (13) which in turn falls until the forces imposed on it by the oil beneath it and the forces imposed on it by its return spring are equal.

In practice, the fuel racks will be fully open to allow the engine to start, the slight delay between the flyweights sensing the increase in speed and the power piston dropping causes the engine speed to increase significantly above idle speed before settling down.

Referring to figure five and figure six, consider a demand to increase the engine speed. The loco power handle in the cab is connected to a valve capable of varying air pressure between 0 psi and 50 psi (3.4 bar); this air pressure sets the 'driver demand' input seen by the 'pneumatic hydraulic actuator' (18 fig 6). This actuator converts the air pressure into oil pressure and produces an output in the form of movement of the governor input lever (23 fig 6).

The input lever acts on the speed control shaft (9 fig 5). which in turn acts on the speed reset valve (10 fig 5). which allows oil to drain from beneath the speed reset piston (3 fig 5). which falls under the influence of oil pressure on the topside of the piston. As the speed reset piston falls it carries with it the floating lever (4 fig 5); this is pivoted on (and thus rotates about) the top of the power piston (13 fig 5). The action of the floating lever falling compresses the speeder spring (11 fig 5). which opens the main pilot valve (16 fig 5). to admit oil to the bottom of the power piston thus raising the power piston against the force of its return spring. The action of the power piston rising rotates the governor output shaft, and therefore the fuel racks, in the increase fuel direction as described above. Governor equilibrium is restored thus; as the power piston rises, the floating lever now pivots about the speed reset piston, this relieves load on the speeder spring and allows the main pilot valve to 'lap' and trap the oil beneath the power piston.

We now have a situation where the engine (and therefore the main generator) is running at full speed (1600 rpm) but producing little output; this is because the main generator field excitation voltage is at minimum. In order to increase generator output the field voltage is increased by cutting out a resistance arranged in series with the field. This is controlled by a 'load regulator' in the form of a rotary switch comprising a number of contacts arranged in a circle. Each contact, when closed, short-circuits a resistor and is closed by a roller attached to a motor controlled (in either an 'increase volts' or 'decrease volts' direction) by the load control contacts on the governor. In reality the generator output is increased at the same time as the engine speed (although not at the same rate).

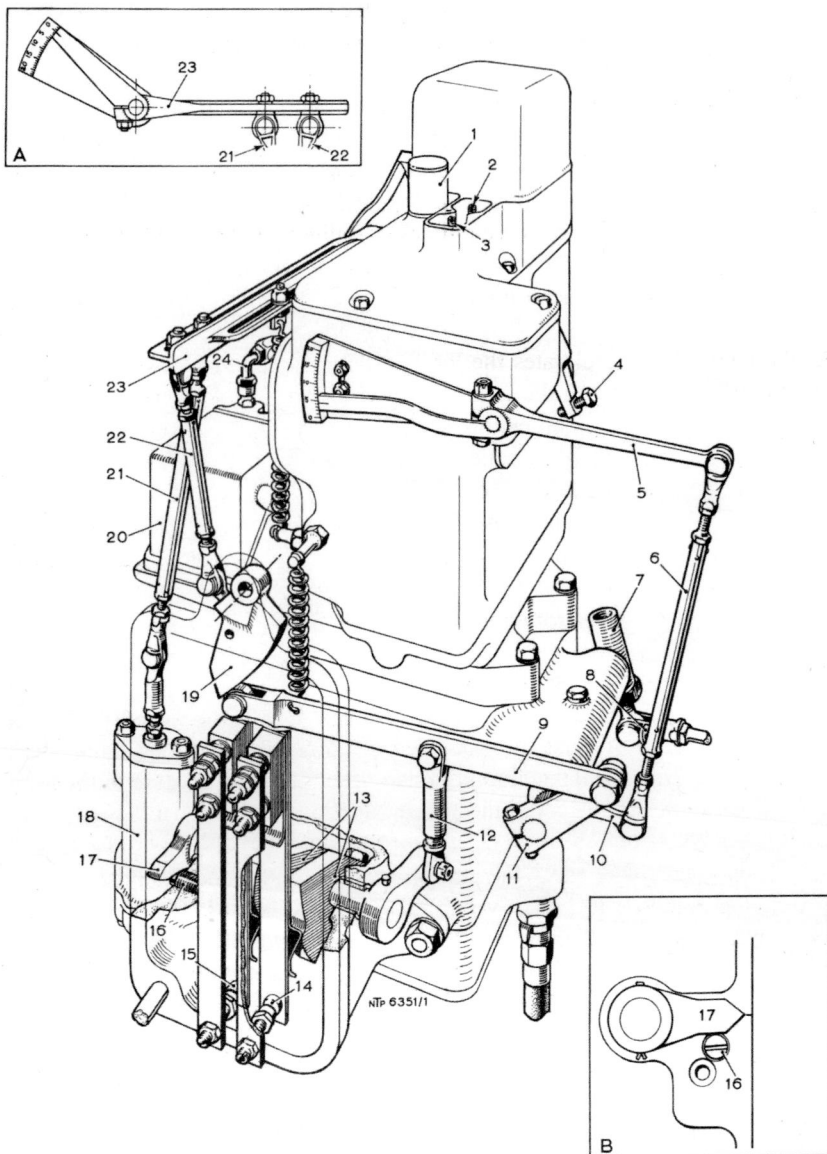

Figure 6. Governor and load control arrangement.

(Referring to figure six) it occurs like this; attached to the input lever (23) is a link (22) which is attached to a cam (19) on the load control switch box. As the input lever moves in the 'increase speed' direction so the cam rotates to allow the differential beam (9) to rise under the influence of its spring, causing the switch cam (13) to close the 'increase load' switch and thus, cutting resistance out of the generator field circuit, increasing generator output. The governor output shaft (5) will rotate because of the actions described previously, as it does so a further link (10) attached to the output lever will act on the opposite end of the differential beam. This will lower the beam and open the 'increase load' switch to stop the increase in generator output.

As the locomotive accelerates the load on the generator decreases and this is sensed by the governor in the form of a slight rise in engine speed. To counter this and attempt to maintain engine speed at its demanded setting the governor will lower the power piston which results in the output lever moving in the 'decrease fuel' direction. Via the linkage previously described this causes the differential beam to rise and close the 'increase load' switch again, as the load increases the engine speed will fall slightly. This fall in speed is sensed by the governor which raises the power piston slightly to increase fuel, this causes the differential lever to fall opening the 'increase load' switch.

The governor and load control system works like this until all the resistance is cut out of the generator field circuit. At this point the load regulator will close a switch to operate the first stage of traction motor field diversion. The whole process is then repeated, the second stage of field diversion occurs in the same manner. A decrease in load has the opposite effect.

In summary, the input from the driver's power handle and, therefore, to the governor is (almost) infinitely variable. The governor will set the fuel rack and load regulator position to give the maximum output for whatever speed is demanded by power handle input.

Certain conditions can cause the engine speed to rise above what is considerable desirable, or safe. To control this is an overspeed device; this is described adequately on page 58.

If a fault condition, or other demand requires the engine to be stopped this is accomplished by de-energising the electrical circuit to the engine run solenoid. This closes the engine run valve within the governor, allows the oil to drain from the underside of the power piston and allows it to fall under the action of its spring to set the fuel rack to the 'no fuel' position. With no fuel being injected, the engine stops.

Photo: Gavin Morrison

The only locomotive that was powered by the Napier T9-29 engine; the English Electric 1100hp Type 2. Representing the class in its original form is D5902 resplendent in ex-works condition at Doncaster Works on 3 May 1959, one day after its formal introduction to traffic. None of these locomotives survive, the final example (D5901) being scrapped at Doncaster in 1977.